The Best Gender-Neutral Baby Name Book

The Best Gender-Neutral Baby Name Book

★ ★ ★ ★

*The Ultimate Collection
of Unique Unisex Names*

MELANIE MANNARINO

TILLER PRESS

New York   London   Toronto   Sydney   New Delhi

TILLER
PRESS

An Imprint of Simon & Schuster, Inc.
1230 Avenue of the Americas
New York, NY 10020

Copyright © 2019 by Simon & Schuster, Inc.

First Tiller Press trade paperback edition July 2019

TILLER PRESS and colophon are trademarks of Simon & Schuster, Inc.

For information about special discounts for bulk purchases, please contact
Simon & Schuster Special Sales at 1-866-506-1949 or business@simonandschuster.com.

The Simon & Schuster Speakers Bureau can bring authors to your live event.
For more information or to book an event, contact the Simon & Schuster Speakers
Bureau at 1-866-248-3049 or visit our website at www.simonspeakers.com.

Interior design by Jaime Putorti

Manufactured in the United States of America

10 9 8 7 6 5 4 3

Library of Congress Cataloging-in-Publication Data is available.

ISBN 978-1-9821-3058-9
ISBN 978-1-9821-3059-6 (ebook)

★ *To Connor Richard:* ★

Your dad and I may have named you,

but only you can decide who you are.

Contents

★ ★ ★ ★

Introduction

Names work *hard*. For generations, they've indicated a lot about people: their family history (in the case of Jr.s, IIs, and IIIs), ethnicity, and personality traits and qualities (let's face it, the name Daisy has never hinted at a strong, outspoken woman)—and let's not forget about nicknames, both good and bad.

But although a name may have special significance to the parents who choose it, when you really think about it, there's little else it can reveal about a baby or the adult that child grows into. In fact, the *only* thing a person's name says about them is what name their parents liked best at the time they were born. No name could ever predict a child's love of ukelele music, their deep dislike of red peppers, or their incredible talent for snapping you out of the worst mood with a quick smile.

That's true now more than ever, especially as gender-neutral baby names have become more popular. Without a traditional "girl name" or "boy name" as a cue, the uniqueness of your baby can shine even brighter. Close your eyes and try to imagine what a kid named "Frankie" looks like. It's difficult, right? He could be a preschool boy who loves "cooking" in his play kitchen or a teenage girl who is the star of her track team. Same goes for Casey, Jamie, Kendall, Peyton . . . gender-neutral names defy stereotyping.

There's no denying this naming trend—15 percent of babies born in 2017 were given gender-neutral names, a number that's nearly doubled in twenty years. We can point to cultural shifts, celebrity influence, a rejection of our own childhoods when there were five Jennifers in one class, and basic personal preference as the cause for the rise. But it's also worth pointing out that not all boy-or-girl names are gender neutral. For example, when was the last time you met a male Leslie under the age of, say, forty? Or a guy of any age named Shannon or Ashley? Despite the cultural turning away from the idea of "girl names" and "boy names," so far the crossover has generally gone only one way, with girls receiving traditional male names—and sometimes, as a result, those names end up firmly in the "girl names" column.

So what is a gender-neutral baby name? It's one that, right now, would serve your baby boy *or* baby girl well. And—as with any baby name worth adding to your short list—it's also one that sounds pleasing to your ears and perhaps makes you think of a beloved family member, friend, public figure, or fictional character. Plus, practically speaking, it's one that you believe your child and others will be able to easily spell and pronounce and that also sounds harmonious with your baby's last name.

We've compiled the best gender-neutral baby names for your child. Use this book as a guide: read it from cover to cover, or dip into certain chapters if you already have a starting letter in mind. Have fun, be creative, and know that whatever name you choose, your baby will be a unique and amazing person who defies assumptions and defines him- or herself.

Top Gender-Neutral Baby Names of 2018

These popular names are topping the charts for boys and girls. (For more about each name, turn to the chapter of the letter it starts with.)

NOAH	EZRA	KINSLEY
LOGAN	EVERLY	ASHER
JAMES	NOVA	
HARPER	QUINN	

Chapter One

Names That Begin with "A"

ABAYOMI: Nigerian, meaning "he has come to bring me happiness" in the Yoruba dialect.

ADAIR: From the ancient Germanic phrase *ead gar*, meaning "wealthy spear."

ADDISON: This name means "Adam's son." (And FYI, Adam means "red earth.")

ADOHI: From a Cherokee word meaning "timber" or "woods."

ADRIAN: From the Latin name Hadrianus, meaning "one from the city of Adria."
Alternate spellings: Adrien, Adrienne, Adriane.

AINSLEY: From the Old English phrase *ansetl leah*, meaning "hermitage clearing." Other possible origins include *an leah* ("only field"), *aegen leah* ("[my] own field"), and *Aegen's leah* (a clearing belonging to someone named Aegen).
Alternate spellings: Ansley, Ainslie.

AKIVA: An alternate form of the Hebrew name Yaakov, meaning "one who trips up another and takes his place."

ALAIN: The French form of Alan. In Gaelic it means "little rock"; in German, it comes from *adal*, which means "precious."
  Alternate spellings: Alayne, Alaine, Alane, Allen.

ALBANY: From the name Alban, which comes from the Latin name Albanus, meaning "white." Other origin theories: This is the Latin version of an ancient tribal name or Gaelic for "rocky crag." Albany is also the capital of New York.

ALCOTT: An Old English name meaning "dweller in an old cottage." It's also the surname of the beloved American author Louisa May Alcott.

ALEK: A nickname of the Russian names Aleksandr and Aleksei, both forms of Alexander, which comes from the Greek name Alexandros, meaning "protector of men."
  Similar names: Alex, Alix, Alec, Alick.

ALI: From an Arabic word meaning "exalted."

ALIJAH: An alternate spelling of Elijah, derived from the Hebrew name Eliyahu, meaning "God is Lord."

ALMOND: More common as a British surname, Almond reportedly appeared as a first name in 1919.

AMARE: African, possibly originating in Ethiopia. Various meanings include "handsome" or "possesses great strength"; translated from the Latin, *amare* means "to love," and in

Hebrew it means "the Lord said." The name recently became popular in the United States because of pro basketball player Amar'e Stoudemire.

Alternate spellings: Amar'e, Amari, Amarey.

Five Food Names That Make Unique Baby Names

APPLE: Popularized in 2004 when the actress/wellness guru Gwyneth Paltrow and the musician Chris Martin gave their daughter this name, it's also a sweet shortcut for the sentiment "apple of our eye."

CLOVE: This seasonal spice is actually the flower bud of a tree native to Indonesia. As a first name, this punchy one-syllable word has a pleasing sound and also contains the word "love."

KALE: Kale's got a reputation as a trendy "it" vegetable, a nutrient-rich leafy green. But the hard "k" and soft "l" sounds work well together, making this name a strong choice for either a boy or a girl.

REESE: It's an arguably irresistible candy, but it's also a traditional surname, giving Reese a history as a gender-neutral name.

SAGE: A Mediterranean plant known for its silvery leaves and savory taste, the word *sage* can also mean "wise." Additionally, burning sage is a centuries-old tradition used to clear negative energies and bring in fresh energy.

AMARI: An African name meaning "possesses great strength"; also a variation of Amar, which means "moon" in Arabic.

AMEN: Inspired by the traditional end of a prayer or hymn, meaning "so be it."

AMES: From the French word *ami,* meaning "friend"; also a variation of the Hebrew name Amos, meaning "carried by the Lord."

AMORY: An alternate spelling of Emory, which comes from the Old English name Emmerich, meaning "home strength," or from the Germanic name Amalrich, meaning "work ruler."
Alternate spellings: Emery, Emory.

ANDY: A nickname of Andrew or Andrea, which come from the Greek name Andreas, meaning "manly."
Alternate spellings: Andi, Andie.

ANGEL: From the Greek name Angelos, meaning "messenger from God."
Similar names: Angelo, Angela, Angelus. In pop culture, it's the name of the early-2000s TV show *Angel,* about a vampire who alternately went by the names Angel and Angelus.

ARBOR: Inspired by nature, trees, and the great outdoors. In the United States, National Arbor Day, which takes place on the last Friday in April, celebrates trees and conservation.

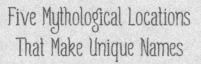

Five Mythological Locations That Make Unique Names

ARCADIA: A mountainous region in ancient Greece known for its pastoral splendor, Arcadia embodies the idea of an idyllic community.

BRASIL: A legendary paradisiacal island off the coast of Ireland that was said to be shrouded in mist and visible only once every seven years.

FINDIAS: One of the four major northern Irish cities of the Tuatha Dé Danann, an ancient race of supernatural beings.

REYNES: The name of a kingdom in the Middle English romance *King Horn,* which dates back to the thirteenth century.

ZION: This name of the hill in Jerusalem where the city of King David was built has come to more generally represent the kingdom of Heaven.

ARDEN: From the Latin phrase *aduenna silva,* meaning "great forest." Arden was the surname of William Shakespeare's mother and of the forest setting of his comedy *As You Like It.*
Alternate spelling: Ardin.

ARI: Traditionally a nickname of Arel and Ariel (from the Hebrew phrase *ari el,* meaning "God's lion") and also Aristotle (from the Greek phrase *aristos totalis,* meaning "the best of all").
Alternate spelling: Arie.

Five Author Surnames
That Make Unique Baby Names

BLAKE: After the nineteenth-century Romantic poet William Blake, perhaps best known for "The Tyger" (you know: "Tyger Tyger, burning bright . . .").

ELLISON: After the American author Ralph Waldo Ellison, whose novel *Invisible Man* won the National Book Award in 1953.

FIELDING: Take your pick: Henry Fielding was an eighteenth-century British author and satirist best known for *Tom Jones*. Fellow Brit Helen Fielding is the author of the 1990s-era *Bridget Jones* books, among others.

SALINGER: After the American author J. D. Salinger, who wrote *The Catcher in the Rye*.

WOOLF: After the twentieth-century British author Virginia Woolf, who wrote *Mrs. Dalloway*, *Orlando*, and other modernist novels.

ARIEL: From the Hebrew phrase *ari el*, meaning "God's lion."
Similar names: Arel, Ari, Arie.

ARLEN: From a Gaelic word meaning "pledge."
Alternate spellings: Arlin, Arlon, Arlan, Arlyn, Erlin.

ARLEY: There are three differing interpretations of this Old English name: "hare wood," "rocky wood," or "eagle wood."

ARLO: Possibly derived from Harlow, from an Old English expression meaning "rocky hill," though some believe it refers specifically to land where armies gather.

Similar names: Arlow, Harlow, Harloe.

ARMEL: A name with French and Celtic origins, derived from Arthmael. Arth means "stone" or "bear"; mael means "disciple," "prince," or "chief."

ARROW: Inspired by the traditional straight-shooting weapon.

ASA: From the Aramaic, meaning "healer."

ASH: Traditionally a nickname of Ashley (from *aesc leah*, meaning "ash grove" in Old English), Ash is now also a stand-alone name that evokes the tree of the same name.

Additional variation: Asher.

ASHTON: From the ancient Germanic phrase *aesc tun*, meaning "ash tree settlement."

Alternate spelling: Ashtyn.

ASPEN: Inspired by the tree of the same name, as well as the popular Colorado ski destination.

ATLANTIS: From an Arabic word meaning "silken." The lost continent of Atlantis is an enduring myth with origins in the Arabic cultures of the Middle East. It was appropriated by the Greeks and probably influenced Welsh and Portuguese mythology as well.

AUBREY: From the ancient Germanic name Alberich, meaning "magical adviser."
Alternate spellings: Aubery, Aubury, Aubary.

AUBURN: Inspired by the reddish-brown shade usually used to describe hair color.

AUGUST: From the Latin name Augustus, meaning "revered." It also refers to the calendar month.

AUSTIN: From the Latin name Augustus, meaning "revered." Also a city in Texas. One alternate spelling, Austen, evokes the nineteenth-century novelist Jane Austen.
Other alternate spellings: Osten, Ostin, Austyn.

AVERILL: From the Old English phrase *eofor hild*, meaning "ferocious fighter."
Alternate spellings: Averil, Averell.

AVERY: A Norman French pronunciation of the English name Alfred, from the ancient Germanic name Aelfraed, meaning "elf counsel."
Alternate spellings: Averie, Averi.

AYAAN: An Islamic name meaning "God's gift."
Alternate spelling: Ayan.

AZARIAH: From the Hebrew name Azarel, meaning "helped by God."

Chapter Two

Names That Begin with "B"

BAAKO: An Akan (West African) expression meaning "first-born child."

BAEZ: A Spanish surname, perhaps most recognizable because of the folk singer Joan Baez.

BAILEY: From an Old English word meaning "bailiff" or "administrative officer," the word may have originated as a local name for someone who lived near a bailey (a city fortification), or it might derive from *beg leah*, meaning "wood clearing."
Alternate spellings: Baileigh, Baylee, Bailee.

BALA: From a Sanskrit word meaning "youngster."
Similar name: Balu.

BALLOU: Likely French, this name sounds like Baloo, a beloved character in Rudyard Kipling's *The Jungle Book*.

BARRY: From the Irish Gaelic name Bearach, meaning "spear." This name is also an anglicized version of Barra, which is a short form of the Irish Gaelic name Fionnbharr, meaning "fair-haired."
Alternate spellings: Bari, Barrie, Bary.

Five Rock Star Names
That Make Unique Baby Names

BOWIE: Most recently, this name has been connected with the musician David Bowie, but historically, it's derived from *buidhe*, a Gaelic word meaning "blond."

DYLAN: This name comes from a Welsh expression meaning "son of the sea." It's also the last name of the outspoken singer-songwriter Bob Dylan.

JAGGER: For a baby name with an edge, look no further than Jagger (rhymes with dagger), after Rolling Stones front man Mick Jagger.

JETT: Derived from the Greek word *gegates*, Jett is the name of a black gemstone originally found in Gagai, a town in Lycia. It is also the surname of the legendary female rocker Joan Jett.

OZZIE: A nickname of Oswald, it's also the name of Ozzie Osbourne, the lead singer of the 1970s heavy-metal band Black Sabbath.

BAY: From the Vietnamese word meaning "seventh"; and commonly given to a child who is born in the seventh month of the year or on the seventh day of the month or week, or who is the seventh child in the family. In English, it could also refer to the aromatic herb or a body of water.

BAYOU: The word comes from the Choctaw word *bayuk*, meaning "small, slow stream," and is most commonly associated with bodies of water in Mississippi and Louisiana.

BEACH: The sandy or rocky shore of an ocean.

BEAN: This name came onto the pop culture radar in the early 1990s, when the musicians Kurt Cobain and Courtney Love named their daughter Frances Bean Cobain. (We don't have to tell you that it's also a popular term of endearment used by parents for babies in utero.)

BECK: A longtime short form of Beckett or Rebecca, Beck also stands on its own, with Norse roots (its source is the Old Norse word *bekkr*, meaning "stream"). The musician Beck Hansen goes by the name Beck professionally, firmly placing the name in American pop culture.

BELLAMY: This name comes from the Old French phrase *bel amy*, meaning "fair friend."

BENTLEY: This name comes from the Old English phrase *beonet leah*, meaning "grass clearing." And, of course, it's also the name of a very expensive automobile.

BERGEN: An ancient Germanic word meaning "mountain."

BERLIN: The name of a city in Germany, divided by a wall from 1961 until 1990.

Five Car Names That Work for Babies, Too

ASPEN: It's a luxury SUV (from Chrysler), as well as a scenic Colorado destination.

ASTON: For auto buffs, the name should conjure the Aston Martin sports car company. But it's also derived from an ancient Germanic expression meaning "settlement in the east."

AUDI: The name of a German car manufacturer, this name is also sometimes used as a nickname for the name Audrey.

DAKOTA: This name is connected to the Native American Dakota tribe and two American states, plus a Dodge pickup truck and a handful of famous people including the actresses Dakota Fanning and Dakota Johnson, the wrestler Dakota Darsow, and NFL quarterback Dakota "Dak" Prescott.

FORD: The surname of the founder of the Ford Motor Company, Ford means "river crossing" in Old English.

BEVIN: This traditional Irish name is based on the Gaelic name Bebhinn, meaning "sweet melody."
Alternate spelling: Bevan.

BILLY: A nickname of Bill, William, and Wilhelmina, from the ancient Germanic phrase *wil helm*, meaning "determined protector."
Alternate spelling: Billie.

BIRCH: From the birch tree, a tree with unique papery bark. The birch has an honored place in American history, according to the Arbor Day Foundation, and has been referenced in poems by Henry Wadsworth Longfellow and Robert Frost.

BIRD: After the animal of the same name.
Alternate spelling: Byrd.

BLAKE: From the Old English word *blaec*, meaning "black"— or, conversely, from the Old English word *blac*, meaning "pale."
Related names: Blakely, Blakeley.

BLAZE: Fires blaze, passion blazes—blaze is an active verb that implies powerful forces at work. The name may also be an alternate spelling of the French name Blaise, which comes from the Latin word *blaesus*, meaning "lisping."

BLUE: This color symbolizes trust and loyalty and has a strong connection to nature (the sky). It is also the name of musician power couple Beyoncé and Jay-Z's first child.

BOBBY: A nickname of Robert and Roberta, which can be traced back to the ancient Germanic name Hredobeorht, meaning "shining with fame."
Alternate spellings: Bobbi, Bobbie.

BRANCH: Like a tree limb, your little one will be a new branch on your family tree.

BRAVERY: A name that indicates strength of character.

BRAZIL: After the South American country of the same name.
Alternate spelling: Brasil.

BRESLIN: An Irish surname.
Alternate spellings: Breaslin, Breslyn, Bresslyn, Breslan, Brezlin, Brezlyn.

BRETT: From the Middle English surname Breton, meaning "one from Brittany."

BRIAR: A shrub or small tree.
Alternate spellings: Bryer, Bryar, Brier, Bryre.

BRIGHTON: Meaning "bright town."
Alternate spellings: Brightyn, Bryton, Britton.

BRILEY: An Irish name meaning "descendant of Roghallach."
Alternate spellings: Brylee, Brylie, Brilee.

BRIO: The definition of brio is "vigor or vivacity"—just the type of characteristic new parents might want to confer on their baby.

BRISTOL: This name can be traced back to the Old English phrase *byrcg stow*, meaning "meeting place by the bridge."
Alternate spellings: Brystol, Bristyl, Bristal.

Nicknames That Make Great Gender-Neutral Baby Names

BERNIE: Short for Bernadette or Bernard, which comes from the ancient Germanic name Beornheard, meaning "strong bear."

CHARLEY: Short for Charles, which comes from the ancient Germanic word *ceorl*, meaning "freeholder." *Alternate spelling:* Charlie.

JACKIE: Short for Jack (itself a nickname of John, from the Hebrew name Yochanan, meaning "God's grace"), Jackson, or Jacqueline.

MATTY: Short for Matilda or Matthew, which comes from the Hebrew name Matityah, meaning "God's gift."

SAM: Short for Samuel and Samantha, both of which come from the Hebrew name Shemuel, meaning "God heard."

BRIXTON: After the district of London.
Alternate spellings: Brixten, Brixtan.

BROOK: From the ancient Germanic word *broka*, meaning "small stream."
Alternate spelling: Brooke; related name: Brooks.

BROOKLYN: After the New York City borough. Famous Brooklyns include the son of the soccer player David Beckham and his wife, Victoria, and the actress Brooklyn Decker.

BRYCE: From the Welsh word *brych*, meaning "dotted."
Alternate spelling: Brice; related name: Bryson.

BRYN: From a Welsh word meaning "hill."
Alternate spellings: Brin, Brynne.

Chapter Three

Names That Begin with "C"

CAELAN: Traditionally an Irish Gaelic boy's name. *Alternate spellings:* Caelen, Caelyn, Calyn.

CAIRO: The capital of Egypt, a city on the Nile River.

CAMDEN: From a Scots Gaelic expression meaning "from the winding." (It's also the location of a Major League Baseball stadium, Oriole Park at Camden Yards, in Baltimore, Maryland.)

Five Major League Stadiums That Could Make Creative Gender-Neutral Baby Names

ANGEL: After Angel Stadium in Anaheim, California.

FENWAY: After Fenway Park, home of the Boston Red Sox.

MARLIN: After Marlins Park in Miami, Florida.

SHEA: After Shea Stadium, the former Queens home of the New York Mets.

WRIGLEY: After Wrigley Field, home of the Chicago Cubs.

CAMERON: From a Gaelic expression meaning "crooked stream," "crooked nose," or "crooked hill." Famous Camerons include the writer-director Cameron Crowe, the actress Cameron Diaz, and NFL quarterback Cameron "Cam" Newton.
Alternate spellings: Camryn, Kameron, Kamryn.

CAMPBELL: From the Gaelic word *caimbeul,* meaning "crooked mouth."

CANYON: After the natural landscape feature, a deep gorge with a river running through it.

CARAWAY: Yes, like the seed, from a plant in the parsley family.

CAREY: From the Gaelic word *car,* meaning "love," or *ciar,* meaning "dark-complected."
Alternate spelling: Cary.

CARLIN: An Irish Gaelic name meaning "little champion."
Alternate spellings: Carlen, Karlin, Karlen.

CARLISLE: From an English word meaning "fortress."
Alternate spelling: Carlyle.

CARRINGTON: An English or Scottish surname, likely from the Old English word *Ceriheringa-tun,* meaning "settlement of Cerihere's people."

CARSON: The origins of this Gaelic name are hazy, but a thirteenth-century form of the name ("de Carsan") hints that it's derived from a place-name. Famous Carsons include the TV host Carson Daly and the novelist Carson McCullers.

CASEY: From the Irish Gaelic name Cathasaigh, meaning "alert."
Alternate spellings: Cacy, Cacey, Caci, Cayci, Caysie, Casie, Kacee, Kacie, Kaci, Kacey, Kaysee, Kacye, Kaycee, Kacy, Kaysie, Kasie, Kayci, Kasee, Kasey, Kaycie.

CASSIDY: From the Irish Gaelic name Caiside, meaning "curly-headed."
Alternate spellings: Cassady, Casidee, Casidy, Kassadi, Kasidy, Kassidie.

CEDAR: From the tall tree known for its timber, oil, and resins.

CHAI: From a Hebrew word meaning "life."

CHANNING: From an English word meaning "wise," though it may also be related to the French word *chanoin*, meaning "churchman."

CHARLIE: A nickname of Charles (from the ancient Germanic word *ceorl*, meaning "freeholder"), this name is frequently used alone.
Alternate spelling: Charley.

Five Tree Names That Would Make Great Baby Names

ASH: In Norse mythology, the ash is known as the "world tree," connecting the heavens, Earth, and the underworld.

BANYAN: This fig tree is native to India and has distinctive branches that grow down into the ground, covering a wide area.

BIRCH: The birch has an honored place in American history, according to the Arbor Day Foundation, and has been referenced in poems by Henry Wadsworth Longfellow and Robert Frost.

CINNAMON: The Ceylon cinnamon tree is native to Sri Lanka.

SEQUOIA: Part of the redwood family, the giant sequoia is the largest tree in the world.

CHAYTAN: From the Sioux word for "hawk."

CHIBEKA: From a Bemba Zambian word meaning "bright one," "shining as the sun," or "shiny."

CHIKO: A Japanese word meaning "arrow" or "pledge."

CHRISTIAN: From a Latin word meaning "Christ's follower."

CLOUD: A weather feature evoking blue skies and softness, stormy weather and rain, and everything in between.

CLOVE: A spice that is actually the flower bud of a tree native to Indonesia.

COBALT: A hard, silvery white magnetic metal, and also an intense shade of blue.

CODY: From an Irish Gaelic word meaning "helper."

COLORADO: Like the western state known for its great outdoors, including the Rocky Mountains and Colorado River.

COMET: A celestial ball of ice and gas that orbits the sun.

CONNELLY: An Irish surname.

COREY: From an Old Norse expression whose meaning has been lost, though some trace it to the name Godfrey, from the ancient Germanic phrase *god fred*, meaning "peaceful god."
Alternate spellings: Cori, Corie, Korey, Kori, Korie.

CORIANDER: The seed of the cilantro herb.

CORIN: From the Latin name Quirinus, meaning "spear."

CREE: A Scottish surname, and also the name of a North American tribe.

CREEK: A body of water similar to a stream, brook, or inlet.

CRUZ: From the Latin word *crux*, meaning "cross."

CYAN: A greenish-blue color.

CYDNEY: From the Old English phrase *sidan eg*, meaning "wide island" or "wide meadow."
  Alternate spellings: Cidney, Sidney, Sydney.

CYPRESS: From an evergreen tree that is adaptable to many climates.

Chapter Four

Names That Begin with "D"

DAI: A nickname of David, this name also means "midwife" in Hindi and "shines" in Welsh.

DAKOTA: The name of a Native American tribe (as well as two US states), it means "allies." Famous Dakotas include the actresses Dakota Fanning and Dakota Johnson, the wrestler Dakota Darsow, and NFL quarterback Dakota "Dak" Prescott.

DALE: Originally a surname that indicated a person who lived in a dale or valley.
Alternate spelling: Dayle.

DALLAS: From the Old English phrase *dael hus*, meaning "house in the valley." Also the well-known Texas city.

DANE: This surname might have indicated Danish ancestry or residence near the English River Dane, or it might be an alternate form of the name Dean.
Alternate spelling: Dayne.

DANI: A nickname of Daniel or Danielle, this name now stands on its own.
Alternate spelling: Danny.

DARIEL: Possibly derived from the name Darrell; see below.

DARIEN: After Darien, Connecticut, and the Darien Gap on the border between Panama and Colombia.
  Alternate spelling: Darian.

DARRAGH: From an Irish Gaelic word meaning "fruitful."

DARRELL: From the French Norman *d'Airel*, meaning "from Airelle" in the Calvados region of France.
  Alternate spellings: Darel, Daryl, Darryll.

DAY: As you might expect, this name comes from the word for the twenty-four-hour period.
Alternate spelling: Dae.

DECEMBER: After the winter month.

DENIM: After the fabric, the name of which comes from *serge de Nimes* ("serge from Nimes"), after the French town where the sturdy fabric was invented.

DENVER: From an Old English expression meaning "Dane's crossing" or "green valley," this is also the name of Colorado's capital.

DEON: From Dionysios, the Greek god of wine, merriment, and theater.
Alternate spellings: Dion, Dionne.

DERRY: From a Gaelic expression meaning "grove of oaks."

DESI: Originally a nickname of Desiderio, which comes from the Latin word *desiderium*, meaning "longing."
Alternate spelling: Dezi.

DESTRY: From the Old French word *destrier*, meaning "warhorse."

DEVIN: From an Old English expression meaning "devotees of Dumnonos," a British tribe that inhabited what is now Devon, England.
Alternate spellings: Devon, Devyn.

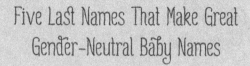

Five Last Names That Make Great Gender-Neutral Baby Names

EASTON: From the Old English phrase *east tun*, meaning "eastern settlement."

LENNOX: From a Scots Gaelic expression meaning "with many elm trees."

MADIGAN: From the Irish Gaelic name Madadhán, meaning "little dog."

MILLER: From an English word meaning "one who grinds grain."

WILEY: From the name of both a village and a river in England.
  Alternate spelling: Wylie.

DEWI: A Welsh version of the name David.

DIAZ: A Spanish surname.

DOMINO: From the Latin word *dominus*, meaning "lord."

DONNELLY: From a Gaelic expression meaning "dark courage."

DORIAN: From a Greek expression meaning "one of the early Greeks."
  Alternate spelling: Dorien.

Five Beach-Related Gender-Neutral Baby Names

ADRIEN: Beachy, but make it French. This name means "from the city of Adria" (on the Adriatic Sea).

RAVI: From a Sanskrit word meaning "sun."

SOL: After the Spanish word for "sun."

SURF: Whether it calls to mind the ocean sport or the refreshing sea spray, surf is a shore thing.

WAVE: May your wave be more tranquil than stormy.

DORSEY: A Norman English surname, meaning "from Orsay."

DREAM: Just like the fantasies that occur during sleep.

DREW: Originally a nickname of Andrew, from Andreas, a Greek name meaning "manly" or "warrior." Famous Drews include the actress Drew Barrymore and the NFL quarterback Drew Brees.
    Alternate spelling: Dru.

DUFF: From the Gaelic word *dubh*, meaning "dark."

DUNE: After the sandy hills of a seashore or desert.

DUSTIN: From the Old Norse name Dorsteinn, meaning "Thor's stone."

DYLAN: From a Welsh expression meaning "son of the sea." Famous Dylans include the actors Dylan McDermott and Dylan Sprouse and the entrepreneur Dylan Lauren.
Alternate spellings: Dillan, Dillon, Dyllun.

Chapter Five

Names That Begin with
"E"

EAGLE: After the bird, known for its keen vision and a powerful symbol in Native American and ancient Roman cultures, among others.

EARLY: From the Old English phrase *earn leah*, meaning "eagle wood" or from *eorlic*, meaning "noble."

EAST: After the direction from which the sun rises.

EASTON: From the Old English phrase *east tun*, meaning "eastern settlement."
Alternate spelling: Eastyn.

EBEN: From a Hebrew word meaning "stone."

ECHO: From the Greek word *ekho*, meaning "reflected sound."

EDDIE: A nickname of many classic names, including Edward, Edwin, Edgar, Edmund, Edwina, and Edna, this name also stands on its own.
Alternate spelling: Eddy.

EDEN: From the Hebrew word *edhen*, meaning "pleasurable place."

Five Gender-Neutral Baby Names Inspired by Animals

FINCH: A songbird with literary connections—in Harper Lee's *To Kill a Mockingbird*, it's the surname of Scout, the story's narrator, and in *The Goldfinch* by Donna Tartt, it is the subject of the titular painting.

FOX: A small omnivorous animal related to wolves, jackals, and dogs, known for its often red fur, clever nature, and pointed ears.

LYNX: A medium-size wildcat with beautiful spotted fur.

ROBIN: A traditional gender-neutral favorite, this is also the name of the American red-breasted bird.

SPARROW: This songbird was a favorite of Aphrodite, the Greek goddess of love.

EGYPT: After the North African country.

EIFEL: A French surname indicating that a person is from Germany's Eifel Mountains. The alternate spelling, Eiffel, is a nod to the Eiffel Tower in Paris, France.

ELEVEN: A master number in numerology (it can be divided only by one and itself), eleven is considered an intuitive number. With a main character called Eleven, the popular TV series *Stranger Things* put this name on the pop-culture map.

ELIF: A name with roots in Turkey (the first letter of the Arabic alphabet) and Norway.

ELIOT: An English derivative of Elias, from the Hebrew name Eliyahu, meaning "God is Lord."
Alternate spellings: Elliot, Elliott.

ELISHA: From a Hebrew expression meaning "God is salvation."
Alternate spelling: Eleisha.

ELLERY: From an Old English expression meaning "alder tree."

ELLINGTON: An English surname indicating that the bearer is from a "settlement associated with Ella."

ELLIS: Like the name Eliot, this name is derived from Elias, from the Hebrew name Eliyahu, meaning "God is Lord."
Similar name: Ellison.

ELM: The strong, sturdy elm tree is mentioned in both Greek and Celtic mythology.

EMBRY: This English surname became popular as a first name thanks to the *Twilight* book series, in which a werewolf is named Embry.

EMERY: From the Old English name Emmerich, meaning "home strength."
Alternate spelling: Emory; *similar name:* Emerson.

Five Gender-Neutral Baby Names
Inspired by Mountains

KAILASH: From the Himalayan mountain, believed to be the paradise of the Hindu god Shiva.

KEA: From Mauna Kea, a dormant volcano on the island of Hawaii that, when measured from its ocean base, is the tallest mountain in the world.

NEVADA: From the Sierra Nevada in the western United States, as well as the Sierra Nevada in Spain. Sierra Nevada means "snow-covered mountains."

RAINIER: From an active volcano in Washington state named after a British naval officer. Native Americans call this mountain Tacoma, which would also make a good baby name, as it means "to surpass" or "to go beyond."

SINAI: From Mount Sinai in Egypt and the Mount Sinai of the Bible, where Moses received the Ten Commandments from God.

ENCINAS: A surname from the Spanish word *encina*, meaning "holm oak," a type of tree.

ENFYS: From a Welsh word meaning "rainbow."

ENZI: A Swahili word that means, among other things, "era," "epoch," "power," or "reign."
Alternate spelling: Enzy.

ENZOKUHLE: Of Zulu/Xhosa origin, meaning "expected to do great things."

ESPEN: A Norwegian name from the Danish word *Åsbjorn*, meaning "god bear" in Danish.

ESSEX: From the Old English phrase "east Seaxe," referring to the English county.

ESTLIN: The middle name of the American poet Edward Estlin "E. E." Cummings.

EVAN: Derived from Euan, from the Gaelic name Eoghan, meaning "youth," as well as the Welsh name Ieuan.
Alternate spellings: Evin, Evyn.

EVER: From the word meaning "at any time" or "at all times."

EVEREST: From the world's highest mountain, in the Himalayas in China and Nepal.

EVERLY: A surname that comes from the Old English words *eofor*, meaning "wild boar," and *leah*, meaning "woodland clearing."

EVIAN: From the spring water or the French town Évian-les-Bains, on Lake Geneva.

EVREN: From a Turkish word meaning "universe" in Turkish.

EZRA: From a Hebrew word meaning "assistance."
Related name: Ezri.

Chapter Six

Names That Begin with "F"

FABLE: A short story with a moral, as in *Aesop's Fables.*

FADHILI: From a Swahili word meaning "kindness."

FAIRFAX: From the Anglo-Saxon *fair feax*, meaning "fair hair."

FALLON: From the Gaelic word *follamhnus*, meaning "superiority."

FARGO: A Spanish surname and also the name of the North Dakota city made famous by a film and TV series of the same name.

FARON: From the Old English phrase *faeger hine*, meaning "handsome servant."
Alternate spellings: Farin, Farran, Farren, Farrin, Farron.

FARRELL: From the Gaelic name O'Fearghail, meaning "descendant of [king] Fearghail."

FEMI: From a Yoruba expression meaning "love me."

FEN: A wetland.
Alternate spelling: Fenn.

Five Gender-Neutral Baby Names Inspired by Movie Titles

KANE: From *Citizen Kane*, Orson Welles's classic 1941 film based on media moguls William Randolph Hearst and Joseph Pulitzer.

MAX: From the postapocalyptic *Mad Max* movies, including the 2015 sequel starring Charlize Theron.

NORTH: When people ask, tell them you got the idea for this name from the Alfred Hitchcock spy thriller *North by Northwest*, starring Cary Grant.

ROCKY: Instill a fighting spirit from the beginning with this nod to the 1970s boxing classic that has spawned five sequels and two spin-offs (to date).

RYAN: From Steven Spielberg's award-winning World War II drama *Saving Private Ryan*.

FENNEL: A vegetable in the carrot family with a distinct licorice taste.

FERRAN: From an Arabic word meaning "baker."
Alternate spellings: Feran, Ferron.

FIFE: Though the original Gaelic meaning has been lost, this name is possibly derived from that of Fib, a son of Cruithne, the legendary father of the ancient people of Britain known as the Picts. A fife is also a small flute played in military bands.
Alternate spelling: Fyfe.

FIFER: From the German word *Pfeiffer*, for someone who plays the fife.
Alternate spelling: Pfeiffer.

FINCH: A songbird with literary connections—in Harper Lee's *To Kill a Mockingbird*, it's the surname of Scout, the story's narrator, and in *The Goldfinch* by Donna Tartt, it is the subject of the titular painting.

FINLEY: From the Scots Gaelic name Fionnlagh, meaning "pure hero."
Alternate spelling: Finlay.

FINN: A name with English, Norwegian, Swedish, and Danish history. Its Scandinavian use is derived from Finnr, an Old Norse name meaning "one from Finland."

FIR: An evergreen tree, some varieties of which are used as Christmas trees. Evergreens symbolize immortality and eternal life because they keep their needles year round.

FIRE: Like the element of nature that burns bright and hot, casting warmth on everything nearby.
Related name: Flame.

FJORD: A deep inlet of the sea situated between high cliffs, created by a glacier.

FLANNERY: From a Gaelic expression meaning "red courage."

FLYNN: From the Irish Gaelic name Flann, meaning "ruddy-complected."

FOREVER: Indicating no end, this name seems just right for a baby you will love now and for all time.

FORREST: An English word for "one who lives by a forest"; this name earned a spot in American pop culture history with the movie *Forrest Gump*.
Alternate spelling: Forest.

Five Gender-Neutral Baby Names Inspired by the Elements

CLAY: From the Old English word *claeg*, meaning "moist earth."

HEAVEN: A place in the sky that many religions believe good people ascend to in the afterlife.

RAIN: Condensed water vapor that falls to Earth.
Alternate spelling: Rainn, like the actor Rainn Wilson.

SPLASH: A water name and the perfect description of the immediate impact babies have on the people around them.

ZEPHYR: A soft, gentle breeze.

FORTUNE: Call it luck, call it serendipity, or call it a windfall. Either way, this name indicates good things.

FOX: This English name was often given as a surname to those with red hair, as well as to those who enjoyed a reputation for cleverness—both as a nod to the animal of the same name.

FRANKIE: Traditionally a nickname of Frances (from an ancient Germanic word meaning "Frenchman"), Francis, Frank, and Franklin, this name now stands on its own.

FREDDIE: Traditionally a nickname of Frederick (from the ancient Germanic phrase *fred ric*, meaning "peaceful ruler"), Wilfred, Freda, and Frederica, this name now stands on its own.

FREE: Unconfined, able to do as one wishes.

FREEDOM: The power or right to do as one pleases.

FRENCH: The adjective for a person from France.

FRIEND: A pal or companion.

FROST: Like the intricate ice crystals. Also the last name of the American poet Robert Frost.

FUTURE: A forward-thinking name for a person who's just coming into the world.

Chapter Seven

Names That Begin with "G"

GAEL: From a Gaelic word meaning "Celt." Famous Gaels include the actor Gael Garcia Bernal and the New York restaurant critic Gael Greene.

GALE: A kind of storm. This classic name landed back on the radar after the success of *The Hunger Games* book and movie series, in which a main character is named Gale.

GALEN: From a Greek word meaning "soothing."

GALWAY: From a Gaelic word meaning "stranger"; also the name of a coastal Irish city.

GARCIA: From the Basque word *artz*, meaning "bear"; this Spanish surname predates the Roman occupation of the Iberian Peninsula.

GARUDA: A bird from Hindu mythology that serves as a vehicle for the god Vishnu.

GAVI: In Hindu, it refers to a forest in Karala. In Hebrew, it's a short form of Gavriel, meaning "God's man."

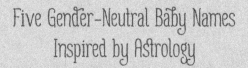

GEMINI: From the Latin word *geminus*, meaning "twins"; this is the astrological sign for people born between May 21 and June 20.

GENESIS: From a Latin word meaning "creation."

GERMAINE: From the Latin name Germanus, meaning "brother."
Alternate spellings: Germain, Germayn, Jermain, Jermaine, Jermayn.

GIANNI: A nickname of the Italian name Giovanni, which is the equivalent of the English name John.

GILI: From a Hebrew expression meaning "my joy."

GINKGO: A native Chinese tree with distinct fan-shaped leaves, the ginkgo is a symbol of longevity and endurance.

GLACIER: A large, slow-moving ice mass. Glaciers have long shaped the landscape of Earth.

GLASGOW: A Scottish surname and city.

GLENN: From the Gaelic word *gleann*, meaning "valley dweller." Famous Glenns include the actress Glenn Close, the actor Glenn Howerton, and the composer Glenn Miller.
Alternate spellings: Glen, Glenne.

GOLDEN: Like the precious metal.

Five Gender-Neutral Baby Names That Translate to "Joy"

ALAITASUN: In Basque.

FARIH: In Arabic.

HARI: In Maori.

ILO: In Finnish.

ÖRÖM: In Hungarian.

Five Gender-Neutral Baby Names Inspired by the Periodic Table of Elements

CARBON: A shape-shifting element, carbon can take the form of soft, dark graphite or crystal-clear, rock-hard diamond.

MERCURY: This element, also known as quicksilver, is named after the fast-moving planet.

NEON: A colorless, inert gas that glows reddish-orange in a vacuum.

SILVER: This precious metal has long been used for currency, jewelry, and household goods.

ZINC: This metal is an essential nutrient for both plants and animals.

GRAY: A surname with English, Scottish, Irish, and French heritage, having to do with gray hair or being from a region named Gray.

Alternate spelling: Grey.

GREEN: From the English word for the color, this was originally a nickname for those who habitually wore green or a surname to identify families who lived near the village green. Among the Irish and Jews, forms of this surname were adopted as a sort of familial ornament, the naming equivalent of putting on bright green clothes.

GROVE: An orchard or small group of trees.

GULL: A coastal bird (seagull).

GUTHRIE: From the Scots Gaelic word *gaothairach*, meaning "windblown place."

Chapter Eight

Names That Begin with "H"

HADAR: From a Hebrew word meaning "glory."

HALCYON: From the Greek word *halkyon*, meaning "kingfisher."

HALE: An Old English and Middle English surname for someone who lived in a nook or hollow.

HALEY: From the Old English phrase *heg leah*, meaning "hay clearing." Famous Haleys include the actor Haley Joel Osment and the singer Haley Reinhart.

HALLOW: Meaning "honor as holy."

HALO: A disc or circle of light around the head of a saint, angel, or other holy person—or around the moon.

HALSEY: An English surname. Famous Halseys include the eponymous singer.

HANAN: From an Arabic word meaning "compassionate."
Alternate spellings: Hannan, Hanon.

HANI: From an Arabic word meaning "happy."

HANIF: From an Arabic word meaning "believer in the truth of Islam."

HARBOR: The name of a place on a coastline that shelters ships.

HARLEM: A neighborhood in New York City known for its renaissance of art and culture in its African American community in the 1920s and '30s.

Five Nautical Gender-Neutral Baby Names

BAY: Like the inlet of the sea. (In Vietnamese this name means "seventh" and is commonly given to a child who is born in the seventh month of the year or on the seventh day of the month or week, or who is the seventh child in the family.)

BLUE: Like the color of both the ocean and the sky.

CREW: After the team that operates a boat or ship. *Alternate spelling:* Crue.

KAI: Hawaiian for "seawater." (In other parts of the world, the name comes from a Greek word meaning "Earth.")

SAILOR: After someone who knows their way around a boat.

HARLEY: From the Old English phrase *hara leah*, meaning "hare wood," or possibly *hoer leah*, meaning "rocky wood."

HARLOW: From an Old English expression meaning "rocky hill."

HARPER: From an English expression meaning "harp player or maker." Famous Harpers include the author Harper Lee and the singer Harper Simon.

HARVEST: From the word used to describe gathering crops, this name has an autumnal feel.

HAVANA: The capital of Cuba.

HAVEN: A place of safety.

HAYDEN: From the ancient Germanic word *heidano*, meaning "heathen."

HAYES: From an Old English word meaning "tall."

HAZE: An alternate spelling of Hayes (see above), a reference to weather-related mist or fog, or a nickname of Hazel.

HEDLEY: From the Old English phrase *haed leah*, meaning "clearing of heather."
Similar name: Hadley.

Five Gender-Neutral Baby Names
That Convey Strength

BRADY: From a Gaelic word meaning "brawny-chested."

CORLISS: From an Old English word meaning "hearty."

EMERY: From the Old English name Emmerich, meaning "home strength," or from the Germanic name Amalrich, meaning "work ruler."
    Alternate spelling: Emory; *similar name:* Emerson.

JELANI: From an African Igbo expression meaning "full of strength."

KEMP: From the Old English word *kempe*, meaning "athlete."

HEIKE: A name with Dutch and German roots, similar to the name Henry or Henrietta.

HENDRIX: Related to the name Hendrick, from the ancient Germanic name Heimrich, meaning "home ruler."

HENLEY: From the Old English phrase *héan leah*, meaning "high wood" or "high clearing."

HOLLIS: After the red-berried holly plant.

HONOVI: From a Hopi word meaning "strong."

HORIZON: The line where the surface of the ground and the sky appear to meet.

HOUSTON: From a Gaelic expression meaning "Hugh's town."

HUDSON: Related to Hugh, a Norman French name meaning "soul."

HUNTER: From the word for one who hunts.

Chapter Nine

Names That Begin with "I"

IDRIS: Its Welsh form is derived from the phrase *iud ris*, meaning "fiery leader." In Urdu, the name comes from an Arabic word meaning "prophet."

IMAN: From an Arabic word meaning "religious leader."

IMRI: From a Hebrew word meaning "eloquent."

INDIANA: After the midwestern state of the same name. Made popular by the movie character Indiana Jones.

INDIGO: A dark-blue color, like the dye that comes from the indigo plant.

INNES: From the Scots Gaelic name Aonghas, meaning "singular choice."

IRA: From a Hebrew word meaning "alert."

IRISH: Referring to someone of Irish descent.

ISA: An alternate form of Isaiah, from the Hebrew name Yeshayahu, meaning "God is my helper."

ISOKE: From an African name meaning "gift from God."

IVORY: From the word for an elephant's tusk or the creamy shade of the same name.

IZZY: Traditionally a nickname of Isidore (from the Greek name Isodorus, meaning "gift from Isis") or Israel (from the Hebrew name Yisrael, meaning "struggles with God"), though it now stands on its own.

Five Gender-Neutral Baby Names Inspired by Movie Icons

BAILEY: From George Bailey, in *It's a Wonderful Life*.

FERRIS: From the clever teen who just wants a break, in *Ferris Bueller's Day Off*.

RIPLEY: From Sigourney Weaver's character in the *Alien* movies.

SPARROW: From Jack Sparrow, from the *Pirates of the Caribbean* movies.

WILLY: From Willy Wonka, of the book and movies by Roald Dahl.

Chapter Ten

Names That Begin with "J"

JACE: Traditionally a nickname of Jason, which comes from the Greek name Iason, meaning "healer."
Alternate spelling: Jayce.

JACEY: A creative take on the initials "JC."
Alternate spelling: Jaycee.

JADEN: Related to the name Jade, after the green mineral used in jewelry, tools, and sculptures.
Alternate spellings: Jadon, Jadin, Jadyn, Jaiden.

JAEL: From a Hebrew word meaning "mountain goat."

JAGGER: From a Middle English surname meaning "carter" or "peddler."

JALEN: A modern name with no particular meaning (it's a blank slate!).
Alternate spellings: Jaylin, Jalyn.

JAMES: From the Latin name Jacomus, meaning "one who trips up another and takes his place."

Five Gender-Neutral Baby Names Inspired by Semiprecious Stones

BERYL: From a mineral known for several of its gemstone varieties, including emerald and aquamarine.

LARIMAR: From a sea blue variety of the mineral pectolite found only in the Dominican Republic.

MALACHITE: From a banded green stone that was one of the first ores used to produce copper.

ONYX: From a solid black chalcedony stone.

PERIDOT: From a yellow-green gem found in lava, meteorites, and the earth's mantle, it is also August's birthstone.

JAMIE: A nickname of James (see above).
Alternate spellings: Jaime, Jayme, Jamey.

JARRELL: An English surname.

JAX: A modern nickname of Jack (itself a nickname of John, from the Hebrew name Yochanan, meaning "God's grace") or Jackson.
Alternate spelling: Jaxx.

JAY: The name of the blue, crested bird, though some believe this name is derived from the Latin name Gaius, meaning

"happy." In Hindi, the name comes from a Sanskrit word meaning "victory."
Alternate spelling: Jae.

JENSEN: A Danish form of the surname Johnson.

JERICHO: From the biblical city, which in Arabic means "city of the moon."
Alternate spelling: Jerico.

JESS: A nickname of Jesse or Jessica.

JESSE: From Yishai, a Hebrew name meaning "gift," or Yaasai, meaning "God lives."
Alternate spelling: Jessie.

JETT: Derived from the Greek word *gegates*, Jett is the name of a black gemstone originally found in Gagai, a town in Lycia.
Alternate spelling: Jet.

JODY: This name is derived from Joseph, from the Hebrew name Yosef, meaning "the Lord's addition [to the family]."

JOEY: A nickname of Joseph (for meaning, see Jody, above), Josephina, or Joel.

JOHNNY: A nickname of John, from Yochanan, a Hebrew name meaning "God's grace."
Alternate spellings: Johnnie, Jonnie, Jonny.

JORDAN: From the Hebrew name Yarden, meaning "flowing down."

Alternate spellings: Jordin, Jordyn, Jourdan.

JORGIE: An alternate spelling of Georgie, a nickname for George (from the Greek name Georgios, meaning "farmer"), Georgette, Georgina, and similar names.

JORI: A nickname of Jordan (see above).

Five Gender-Neutral Baby Names Inspired by Famous Rivers

AMUR: From an East Asian river that flows through Russia, Mongolia, and China. Its Chinese name means "Black Dragon River."

DANUBE: From a European river that starts in Germany and ends in the Black Sea, passing through ten countries on its way.

EUPHRATES: From a Greek phrase meaning "sweet water."

NILE: From a north-flowing river in northern Africa, it is the longest river in the world.

THAMES: From the British river often referred to as London's oldest highway, because of its key role in trade and commerce.

JOSS: Possibly a nickname of Joshua, which comes from the Hebrew name Yehoshua, meaning "God is salvation."

JOURNEY: From the word for a trip or voyage.

JUDE: From the Hebrew name Yehudah, meaning "praise."

JULES: A nickname of Julian, which comes from the Latin name Julianus, meaning "Jove's descendant."

JUSTICE: From the word meaning fair behavior or treatment.

Chapter Eleven

Names That Begin with "K"

KACEY: An alternate spelling of Casey, which comes from Cathasaigh, an Irish Gaelic name meaning "alert."
Alternate spellings: Cacy, Cacey, Caci, Cayci, Caysie, Casie, Kacee, Kacie, Kaci, Kaysee, Kacye, Kaycee, Kacy, Kaysie, Kasie, Kayci, Kasee, Kasey, Kaycie.

KADEN: From an Arabic expression meaning "companion."
Alternate spellings: Caden, Kadin, Kadyn, Kaedin, Kayden.

KAEDE: The name of a Japanese maple tree and also an alternate spelling of Cade, which comes from an Old French word meaning "cask."
Additional variation: Kade.

KAELAN: From the Irish Gaelic name Caolan, meaning "slim."
Alternate spellings: Kalen, Kellan.

KAI: This name means different things in different cultures. In Greek, it means "Earth"; in Hawaiian, it means "seawater"; and depending on the tone and character associated with the name, its Chinese meaning can be "victorious," "open," "start," or "ideal."

Five Gender-Neutral Hindu and Buddhist-Related Baby Names

BRAHMA: From the Sanskrit word *brahman*, meaning "prayer." In Hinduism, Brahma is the creator of the universe.

DEVEN: From a name of the god Indra.

JITENDRA: From a Sanskrit expression meaning "Indra's conqueror."
Related name: Jeetendra.

KALIDAS: From the Sanskrit phrase *kali dasa*, meaning "servant of the goddess Kali" (a wife of the Hindu god Shiva).

TULSI: From a Sanskrit word meaning "sacred basil."

KAILASH: From a Sanskrit expression whose meaning has been lost; this is also the name of a mountain in the Himalayas that is said to be the site of the god Shiva's paradise.

KALAN: An alternate spelling of Callan, which comes from a German word meaning "chatter."
Additional variations: Kallan, Kallen.

KAMRAN: From a Gaelic expression meaning "crooked stream," "crooked nose," or "crooked hill."
Alternate spellings: Cameron, Camryn.

KANE: From the Irish Gaelic name Cathan, meaning "battler." *Alternate spelling:* Kayne.

KASEN: This name is derived from Casey, which comes from Irish Gaelic name Cathasaigh, meaning "alert." *Alternate spellings:* Casen, Cason, Kacen, Kason, Kaysen, Kayson.

KAZUMI: From a Japanese name meaning "beautiful peace."

KEATON: An English surname indicating that a person was from the region of Keaton.

KEEGAN: From the Gaelic name Aodhagan, meaning "small flame." *Alternate spellings:* Keagan, Kegan.

KEELAN: From the Gaelic name Caoilinn, meaning "slim and fair." *Alternate spellings:* Keelin, Keilan.

KEHINDE: From a Yoruba expression meaning "person who falls behind"; this name is traditionally given to the second born of twins.

KELBY: From a Gaelic word meaning "place by the flowing water."

KELECHI: From an Igbo name meaning "thank God."

Five Gender-Neutral Japanese Baby Names

HINATA: "Sunny place."

MAKOTO: "True."

NAO: "Honesty."

REN: "Lotus" or "love."

YASU: "Peace," "quiet," or "calm."

KENDALL: From the ancient Germanic word Kentdale, meaning "Kent river valley."

KENNEDY: From the Irish Gaelic name Cinneidigh, meaning "helmet head."

KENYA: From a Kiswahili expression whose meaning has been lost, this name is often given in honor of the East African country of the same name, itself named after the second-tallest mountain peak in Africa.

KERR: From the Old Norse word *kjarr*, meaning "overgrown marsh."

KHARI: From a Kiswahili word meaning "kingly."

KIERAN: From the Irish Gaelic name Ciaran, meaning "black-haired."

Alternate spellings: Kieren, Kieron, Kyran; related name: Kiernan.

KILLIAN: From the Irish Gaelic name Ceallach, meaning "brilliant hair."
Alternate spelling: Kilian.

KINDRED: From the word for "family."

KINGSLEY: From the Old English name Cyningesleah, meaning "king's wood."
Additional variation: Kinsley.

KITT: Traditionally a nickname of Christian (from the Latin name Christianus, meaning "one who follows Christ") or Christopher (from the Greek name Kristophoros, meaning "Christ carrier").

KIYOTO: A Japanese name represented by characters that mean "clear person."

KLEE: From the Middle High German word *Kle*, meaning "clover."

KODY: From an Irish Gaelic word meaning "helper."
Alternate spellings: Codey, Coady, Codie, Codi, Kodie, Kodi, Kodee.

KOI: From a Choctaw word meaning "panther"; also the Japanese word for "carp."

KOREY: An alternate spelling of Corey, which comes from an Old Norse expression whose meaning has been lost, though some trace it to the name Godfrey, from the ancient Germanic phrase *god fred*, meaning "peaceful god."
Alternate spellings: Cori, Corie, Corey, Kori, Korie.

KRISHNA: From the Sanskrit word *krsna*, meaning "dark." Krishna is a major Hindu deity, the eighth incarnation of Vishnu, the god of protection.

KYLAN: An alternate form of the name Kyle (see below).
Alternate spelling: Kylen.

KYLE: From the Gaelic word *caol*, meaning "narrow" or "straight." Famous Kyles include the reality star Kyle Richards, NASCAR driver Kyle Busch, and NBA player Kyle Lowry.
Alternate spellings: Cyle, Kile, Kiel.

KYLER: From a Dutch word meaning "archer."

Chapter Twelve

Names That Begin with "L"

LAKE: After the body of water surrounded by land.

LAKOTA: After the Native American people of western South Dakota.

LAND: Either refers to the earth beneath our feet or is a nickname of Landon (see below).

LANDON: From the Old English phrase *lang dun*, meaning "long hill" or "ridge."

LANE: A surname used to designate those who lived near a path or lane, it also represents the convergent development of the Old French name Laine (wool), given to those in the wool trade, and the Gaelic names Luan (warrior) and Laighean (spear).

LANGLEY: From the Old Norse name Langlíf, meaning "long life."

LARIMAR: From a sea-blue variety of the mineral pectolite found only in the Dominican Republic.

LARK: From a songbird that sings while flying.

LARKIN: From a Gaelic word meaning "fierce"; related to Lorcan.

LARKSPUR: From the flower of those born in July, with tall rows of colorful petals.

LAZULI: From lapis lazuli, a deep-blue mineral used in jewelry.

LEAF: From the English word.

Five Gender-Neutral Baby Names Inspired by Trees

BRANCH: Like a tree limb, your little one will be a new branch on your family tree.

FOREST: From the name for a large group of trees; the word conjures an entire biosphere of animals and plant life.
   Alternate spelling: Forrest.

GROVE: From an orchard or small group of trees.

MOSS: Like the soft green plant that grows in carpets in the shade of trees.

TIMBER: Evoking the names Tim and Kimberly; also a nod to the wood made from trees for building.

LEAL: From the word meaning "loyal" and "honest."

LEE: From an Old English word meaning "meadow."

LEGACY: From the word meaning something you leave behind for others.

LEGEND: From the word meaning a well-known story that may or may not be true; also, a person who is famous for a certain action or quality.

LEIGHTON: From the Old English phrase *leac tun*, meaning "leek settlement."

LEITH: A Scottish surname indicating the town a person was from.

LEMON: From the bright-yellow, tart citrus fruit.

LENNON: From a Gaelic word meaning "little cloak."

LENNOX: From a Scots Gaelic expression meaning "with many elm trees."

LEONE: From the Latin word meaning "lion."

LEX: Short for Alexander or Alexandra (and all related names), which comes from the Greek name Alexandros, meaning "protector of men."

LIGHT: From the English word, which implies the sun, weightlessness, and all other positives associated with the word.

LINDEN: From the Old English phrase *lind dun*, meaning "lime tree hill."

LOGAN: From the Gaelic word *lag*, meaning "hollow." In Chinese, it means "little hollow."

LOKI: From the name of a trickster god from Norse mythology whose name likely means "knot" or "tangle."

LONDON: From an English surname for those from London or those who traveled to London regularly.
Alternate spelling: Londyn.

LOU: Traditionally a nickname of Louise or Louis, both derived from the ancient Germanic name Hlutwig, meaning "famous warrior."

LOXLEY: An English surname indicating the town a person was from.
Alternate spelling: Locksley.

LOYAL: From the word for someone who is true to a person or cause.

LOYALTY: From the word meaning the act of being loyal.

Five Gender-Neutral Baby Names from Classic Children's Literature

CHARLIE: From the sweet and deserving hero in Roald Dahl's *Charlie and the Chocolate Factory* and *Charlie and the Great Glass Elevator*.

JAMIE: From one-half of the museum-squatting, mystery-solving sibling duo in *From the Mixed-Up Files of Mrs. Basil E. Frankweiler*, by E. L. Konigsburg.

MAX: From the imaginative imp from Maurice Sendak's *Where the Wild Things Are*.

ROBIN: From Christopher Robin, Winnie the Pooh's gentle human friend in *Winnie-the-Pooh* by A. A. Milne.

SCOUT: From the astute young narrator in Harper Lee's *To Kill a Mockingbird*.

LUCA: The Italian version of Lucas, which comes from the Greek name Loukas, meaning "one from Lucania."

LUCKY: From the word for being, having, or bringing good luck.

LUMEN: For a word meaning a measurement of light.

LYLE: Originally a name for someone who lived on an island (from the Old French word *l'isle*). In classic children's literature, it's the name of a New York City town house–dwelling crocodile.

LYNX: From the medium-size wildcat with a spotted coat.

LYRIC: From the words of a poem or a song.

Chapter Thirteen

Names That Begin with "M"

MAAYAN: From a Hebrew expression meaning "water source."

MACK: From a Gaelic expression meaning "son of."

MACKENZIE: From the Scots Gaelic name Kenneth, meaning "fire-born."

MADIGAN: From the Gaelic name Madadhán, meaning "little dog."

MAGEE: An anglicized version of McGee, from the Gaelic name Mac Aodha, meaning "son of Aodha."
   Related name: McGee.

MAGIC: From the word for supernatural, mystical, or unexplained actions. Made popular by NBA player Magic Johnson.

MAI: Depending on the Chinese character used to represent this name, it can mean "moving forward with big strides" or "wheat."

MAILLOL: From the French artist and sculptor Aristide Maillol.

Five Otherworldly Gender-Neutral Names

FINN: From Finn MacCool, a mythical Irish warrior.

HERO: From a priestess of the Greek goddess Aphrodite.

IMAN: From a faith in the metaphysical aspects of Islam.

PHOENIX: From a Greek mythological bird that dies aflame and is reborn from the ashes.

RUNE: From a symbol of mysterious or magical importance.

MAINE: From the northeastern US state, famous for its blueberries and lobster.

MAITLAND: A Scottish and English surname, the meaning of which is unknown.

MAIZE: From the Spanish word for "corn."

MAKO: From the Hungarian name Makó, which comes from the Greek name Makarios, meaning "blessed"; also a Japanese name that means either "is true" or "tiger" depending on the character used. It is also a type of shark.

MALAK: From an Arabic word meaning "angel," this name

shares a common ancestor with the Hebrew source that gave us the English name Malachi.

MANUKA: From the name of a bush in New Zealand and also of the honey that comes from the bees that pollinate the plant.

MANUKU: From a Hawaiian expression meaning "like a bird."

MARCH: From the third month of the year, known to come in like a lion and go out like a lamb, which was named after Mars, the Roman god of war.

MARLEY: From an Old English phrase meaning "pleasant," "pine," or "woodland clearing." Famous Marleys include the singer Marley Shelton and the DJ Marley Marl.

MARLOW: From the Old English phrase *mere lafe*, meaning "driftwood."

MARS: From the name of the fourth planet in the solar system, named after the Roman god of war.

MARSH: A nickname for Marshall, which comes from the ancient Germanic phrase *marah scalc*, meaning "horse keeper"; this name could also refer to wetlands.

MATISSE: From the French artist Henri Matisse, known for his use of color.

MATTY: A nickname of Matthew, which comes from the Hebrew name Matityah, meaning "God's gift."
Alternate spellings: Maddy, Maddie, Mattie.

MAURY: A nickname of Maurice, which comes from the Latin name Mauricus, meaning "dark-complected."

MAX: From the Latin name Maximilianus, meaning "the greatest."

McKINLEY: From the Gaelic name Mac Fhionnlaoich, meaning "son of the white warrior."

MEAD: From the Middle English word *mede*, meaning "meadow." It's also an alcoholic beverage fermented from honey.
Alternate spelling: Meade.

MEL: Traditionally a nickname of Melvin, Melvina, Melanie, Melissa, Melody, and Melinda. Famous Mels include 1990s Spice Girls bandmates Mel B and Mel C, the singer Mel Tormé, and the director Mel Brooks.

MEMPHIS: The ancient capital of Egypt, at one time called Men-nefer, meaning "enduring and beautiful," and adapted to "Memphis" by the Greeks. It is also a city in Tennessee known for being the home of the blues.

MERCER: A surname from the Old French word *mercier* or *merchier*, meaning "merchant."

MERCURY: From the Latin name Mercurius, meaning "commerce." This name is also sometimes a nickname for a fleet-footed runner.

MERIDIAN: A circle on the planet that passes longitudinally through the poles; also, one of twelve energy (*qi*) pathways on the body in Chinese medicine.

MERLE: From an Old French word meaning "blackbird" or from the Irish Gaelic name Muirgheal and the Scots Gaelic name Muireall, both meaning "sparkling sea." Famous Merles include the actress Merle Dandridge and the late country singer Merle Haggard.

MESSIAH: From the word for a leader or savior.

METEOR: A small particle of matter that creates a streak of light as it shoots through the sky.

MICAH: Related to the name Micha (see below). In the Jewish scriptures, it was the name of a prophet who warned the Jewish people of imminent invasion and ruin.

MICHA: From a Hebrew name meaning "who is like God."

MICKEY: A nickname of Michael and Michaela, both of which come from the Hebrew name Micha (see above).

MIDNIGHT: A time of day (12:00 a.m.); also often used to indicate a dark, almost black color (think: midnight blue).

MIKKO: A form of Michael.
   Alternate spellings: Miko, Mico.

MILAN: From the Latin family name Aemilianus, meaning "eager," "laborious," or "rival." Its use among Hindi speakers is derived from a Sanskrit expression meaning "a coming together."

MINK: From the Dutch word *meine*, meaning "powerful" or "strong." Also the name of a semiaquatic animal known for its lustrous fur.

MITRA: A Hindu god that represents friendship, integrity, and harmony.

MONACO: A European principality near France; also an Italian surname derived from the word for "monk."

MONTANA: From a Latin word meaning "mountain"; also the name of a western US state.

MOON: After Earth's moon, which exerts a gravitational pull on our planet. Also from a Korean word meaning "educated."

MORGAN: From a Welsh expression meaning "circling sea" or another phrase, *mawr can*, meaning "great brightness." Famous Morgans include the actor Morgan Freeman and the professional beach volleyball player Morgan Beck Miller.

MOROCCO: From an Arabic word for "western kingdom" or "the west"; the name of a country in northern Africa.

MOSI: From a Kiswahili expression meaning "first-born."

MOSS: Related to the name Moses, from the Hebrew name Moshe, meaning "savior"; this is also the word for the soft green plant that grows in carpets in the shade of trees.

MUNRO: A Scots Gaelic name meaning "mouth of the river Rotha [in Ireland]."
Alternate spellings: Monro, Monroe.

MURPHY: From the Irish Gaelic name Murchad, meaning "sea warrior."

Chapter Fourteen

Names That Begin with "N"

NAIROBI: After the city in Kenya, which is named after the Nairobi River. The name comes from the Masai phrase *enkare nyrobi*, meaning "cold water."

NASEEM: From an Urdu name that comes from an Arabic word meaning "breeze."
Alternate spellings: Nasim, Nassim, Nesim, Nessim.

NAT: Traditionally a nickname for Natalie (from a Latin name meaning "the Lord's birthday"), Nathan (from the Hebrew name Natan, meaning "he has bestowed"), and Nathaniel (from the Hebrew name Netanyahu, meaning "God has given").

NATURE: From the word for the plants, animals, and other nonhuman life on Earth.

NAVY: From the dark-blue color or the sea-based branch of the armed services.

NEAL: From the Irish Gaelic name Niall, meaning "champion." Other possible meanings include "cloud" and "passionate."
Alternate spellings: Neale, Neil, Neel.

Five Gender-Neutral Names
Inspired by Sci-Fi Movies

ANAKIN: George Lucas invented this name for the *Star Wars* saga—back in 1974, in his first draft of the script—though it wasn't on the mainstream radar until 1999's *The Phantom Menace* was released.

ARTEMIS: From the Greek goddess of the hunt, Artemis is also the male title character in the movie adaptation of the popular children's book series *Artemis Fowl*.

FOX: From alien seeker Fox Mulder of TV's *The X-Files* (which also inspired two movies).

MARTY: From the name of 1980s time traveler Marty McFly, from the *Back to the Future* movies.

RORY: One of Dr. Who's companions, Rory appeared in the series of the same name.

NEO: Thank the late-1990s sci-fi hit *The Matrix* for bringing this name to the masses. Neo is an anagram for "one."

NEVADA: From a Spanish word meaning "snowfall"; also the name of a southwestern US state.

NICKY: Traditionally a nickname of Nicole and Nicholas (both from the Greek name Nikolaos, meaning "victorious people").
Alternate spellings: Nicki, Nikki, Nickey, Nickie, Nicci.

Five Gender-Neutral Names
Inspired by Winter

FROST: After the delicate white ice crystals that form on blades of grass, windows, and elsewhere.

STORM: More poetic than *blizzard*, this name conjures a force to be reckoned with (and maybe also the cozy trappings of a snowstorm, such as a roaring fire and a mug of hot cocoa).

VAIL: From the Colorado ski destination.

WINTER: Perfect for a baby born between the winter solstice (December 21) and the spring equinox (March 20).

YULE: From an Old English word meaning "Christmas-time."

NICO: Like Nicky (see above), this is a nickname for Nicole and Nicholas.

NIGHT: From the time of day.

NILE: An alternate form of Neil and Niles (both from Niall, an Irish Gaelic name meaning "champion"); also a major river running through Egypt.

NOAH: From the Hebrew name Noach, meaning "peaceful";

other interpretations are "long-lived," "comforter," and "wanderer."

Alternate spelling: Noa.

NOBLE: From the Latin word *nobilis*, meaning "high-born."

NOE: A nickname of Noah (see above).

NOOR: From an Arabic word meaning "light."

NORRIE: A nickname of Noah (see above).

NORTH: After the direction in which a compass needle points. Famous Norths include North West, daughter of the reality star Kim Kardashian and the singer Kanye West.

NOVA: From a Latin word meaning "new."

NOVEMBER: The name of the eleventh month comes from the Latin word for "nine."

Chapter Fifteen

Names That Begin with "O"

OAK: From the tree, known for its hard wood and acorns and symbolizing strength.

OAKLEY: From the Old English phrase *ac leah*, meaning "oak tree clearing."

OBERON: An alternate spelling of Auberon, which comes from the ancient Germanic name Adalbero, meaning "royal bear."

OCEAN: From one of the five oceans, which cover 70 percent of the planet.

ODE: From a poem addressed to a particular person.

OLEANDER: A flowering shrub with a name that sounds similar to the name Leander, which comes from the Greek name Leandros, meaning "lion man."

OLLIE: Traditionally a nickname of Olivia (from the Latin name Oliva, meaning "olive") or Oliver (from the French name Olivier, meaning "olive tree").

OMEGA: From a Greek word meaning "the end," it is the last letter of the Greek alphabet.

ONYX: A solid black chalcedony stone.

ORIEL: An alternate spelling of Auriel, from a Latin word meaning "golden."

ORION: A hunter in Greek mythology; also, the constellation that bears his name.

Five Poetic Gender-Neutral Names

BALLAD: From the name of a poem or song that tells a story, often handed down orally.

HAIKU: From the name of a Japanese poem of seventeen syllables in three lines of five, seven, and five syllables, respectively.

LYRIC: From the name for the words of a poem or song.

POET: From the word for one who creates poetry.

SONNET: From the name of a poem of fourteen lines with ten syllables per line.

Chapter Sixteen

Names That Begin with
"P"

PACE: From the Hebrew word Pesach, meaning "Passover."
Alternate version: Pacey.

PADGET: From a Middle English word for "page" or "young attendant."
Alternate spelling: Padgett.

PAINTER: From the word for an artist who paints pictures.

PALI: A nickname of Palila, from a Hawaiian word meaning "bird."

PALMER: From an English word meaning "pilgrim," it referred to the palm branch carried by a Christian pilgrim while traveling to a holy shrine.

PARKER: From an English word meaning "park keeper."

PASCAL: From the Latin name Paschalis, meaning "Easter child."
Alternate spelling: Pascale.

PASCOE: A nickname of Pascal (see above).
Alternate spelling: Pasco.

PAX: From the Latin word for "peace"; also the name of the Roman goddess of peace.

PAYSON: An English surname meaning "son of peace."
Alternate spellings: Paysen, Peyson, Pacyn, Pason.

PAYTON: An Old English surname indicating that a person was from "Pœga's town."
Alternate spellings: Paityn, Peighton, Peyton.

PAZ: From a Spanish word meaning "peace."

PEACE: From the English word meaning harmony and tranquility.

PENN: From an Old English word meaning "hill."

Five Gender-Neutral Names That Mean "Peace"

ACHUKMA: From Native American Choctaw.

AMAHORO: From Kirundi (Burundi).

FRIEDE: From German.

HÁLÁ: From West African Mawu.

MÍR: From Czech.

PEPPER: A nickname for an energetic, fast-paced person (from the word "pep," perhaps). Also a vegetable and seasoning.

PEREGRINE: From the Latin name Peregrinus, meaning "wanderer"; also the name of a fast-flying bird of prey.

PERRIN: A nickname of Pierre, from the Greek name Petros, meaning "rock."

PERRY: A nickname of Peregrine (see above) or a name that comes from the Old English word *perige*, signifying a person who lived or worked around a pear tree.
Alternate spellings: Peri, Perri, Perrie.

PERU: After the South American country that was the center of the Incan Empire.

PHILADELPHIA: The city of brotherly love (both in the New Testament and in Pennsylvania).

PHOENIX: From the Greek word *phoinix*, meaning "dark red"; the name of a Greek mythological bird that dies aflame and is reborn from the ashes.

PITCH: From the English word for the highness or lowness of a tone, the steepness of a slope, or a throw (like a baseball pitch).

POE: From the surname of Edgar Allan Poe, an American writer famous for his tales of mystery and horror.

Alternate spelling: Po.

POET: From the word for one who creates poetry.

PORTER: From an English word meaning "gatekeeper" and also the French verb *porter*, meaning "to carry."

PRESLEY: From the Old English phrase *preost leah*, meaning "priest's field." Also the surname of the American music icon Elvis Presley.

Five Gender-Neutral Names Inspired by American Icons

JESSE: From Jesse Owens, a track and field athlete and four-time gold medalist in the 1936 Olympics.

MONROE: From the 1950s actress Marilyn Monroe.

TAYLOR: From the musician Taylor Swift.

TRUTH: From Sojourner Truth, an abolitionist and women's rights activist who was born into slavery.

WINFREY: From the influential media mogul Oprah Winfrey.

Chapter Seventeen

Names That Begin with "Q"

QHAMA: From a Xhosa word meaning "fruitful."

QI: In Chinese, depending on the tone and character, it can mean "enlightenment," "to open," "to rise," "to build," or "to begin."

QUANT: A surname from the Middle English word *cointe*, meaning "cunning," "crafty," "knowledgeable," or "attractive," or the Old French word *quointe*, meaning "knowing" or "clever."

QUASIM: From an Arabic expression meaning "one who shares."

QUELL: From the word meaning to calm, soothe, or quiet.

QUILL: From the Gaelic name Coll, meaning "hazel tree."

QUILLAN: A surname that traces back to northern Ireland.

QUIMBY: An English surname based on location, possibly for someone from Quarmby or Quenby.

QUINCY: From a Norman French expression meaning "Quintus's estate."

Alternate spelling: Quincey.

QUINLAN: From the Gaelic surname O'Caoindealbhain, meaning "descendent of Caoindealbhain."

QUINN: From the Irish Gaelic name Conn, meaning "wise leader."

Alternate spelling: Quin.

Chapter Eighteen

Names That Begin with
"R"

RABI: From an Arabic word meaning "breeze."

RAIN: From the word for water that falls from the sky in drops. *Alternate spellings:* Raine, Rayn, Rayne; similar names: Reign, Rein, Reine.

RALEIGH: From the Old English phrase *ray leah*, meaning "deer meadow."

RANDY: From an ancient Germanic word meaning "shield."

RAVEN: After the black bird of the same name, made famous in Edgar Allan Poe's poem "The Raven."

RAY: A nickname of Raymond, from the ancient Germanic phrase *ragin mund*, meaning "protecting hands." *Alternate spellings:* Rae, Rey.

RAZA: From an Arabic word meaning "contentment."

READ: From an Old English word meaning "red." *Alternate spellings:* Reide, Reade, Reid, Reed.

REAGAN: From the Gaelic name Ríagáin, which is thought to come from *ríodhgach*, meaning "impulsive" or "furious."
Alternate spellings: Raegan, Regan.

REASON: From the word for an explanation or justification or a human's ability to think logically.

REBEL: From the word for someone who rises in resistance against authority or the status quo. One famous Rebel is the actress Rebel Wilson.

RED: Traditionally a nickname given to people with red hair.

REECE: From the Welsh name Rhys, meaning "enthusiasm."
Alternate spellings: Reese, Rhys.

REEVE: From an Old English expression meaning "bailiff" or "steward."

REIN: From the ancient Germanic word *ragin*, meaning "advice."
Alternate spelling: Reine; similar names: Raine, Rayn, Rayne, Reign.

REMI: A variation of the French name Rémy, from the Latin name Remigius, meaning "oarsman."

REN: From a Japanese word meaning "lotus" or "love," depending on the character.

REY: From a Spanish word meaning "king." Also the name of the female hero in *Star Wars: The Force Awakens*.
Alternate spelling: Ray.

RHETT: From the Latin word *rhetor*, meaning "speaker"; this surname became popular as a first name after the 1936 publication of Margaret Mitchell's book *Gone with the Wind*—and the subsequent movie—introduced the character Rhett Butler to pop culture.

RHYS: From a Welsh word meaning "enthusiasm."
Alternate spellings: Reece, Reese.

RIDLEY: From the Old English phrase *hreod leah*, meaning "reed clearing."

RILEY: From the Old English phrase *ryge leah*, meaning "rye clearing."
Alternate spellings: Reilly, Ryleigh, Rylee.

RIO: From the Spanish word *río*, meaning "river." Also the short name of the Brazilian city Rio de Janeiro.

RIPLEY: An English surname from the Old English words *ripel* and *leah*, meaning "strip of land," "wood," or "clearing." Also the nickname and surname of the heroine of the *Alien* movies, Ellen Ripley.

RISHI: From a Hindu name meaning "pleasure," "ray of light," "wise," or "pious."

RIVER: From the word for a large stream of water that flows into another body of water. Famous Rivers include the actor River Phoenix and the social media star River Bleu.

ROBIN: A nickname of Robert, from the ancient Germanic name Hreodbeorht, meaning "shining with fame."
Alternate spelling: Robyn.

ROCKET: From the word for a projectile, such as a firework or spaceship.

ROGUE: From the word for someone who breaks away from the pack or the standard way of doing things.

ROHAN: From the Sanskrit word *rohana*, meaning "rising."

ROME: From the ancient Roman empire, a historic Italian city.

ROMY: A nickname of Rosemary or Romulus, the legendary founder with his twin brother, Remus, and first king of the city of Rome.

RONNIE: A nickname of Aaron (from the Hebrew word *haron*, meaning "mountain of strength"), Ronald (from the Old Norse name Rögnvaldr, meaning "ruler's counselor"), and Veronica (from the Greek name Berenike, meaning "bringer of victory").
Alternate spellings: Roni, Ronni, Ronny.

Five Gender-Neutral Names
Inspired by Outer Space

ECLIPSE: From the word for a phenomenon in which the moon passes between the earth and the sun, creating a solar eclipse, or the earth passes between the sun and the moon, creating a lunar eclipse.

GALAXY: From the word for a vast system of stars and planets held together by gravitational force.

HALO: From the word for a circle of light around the sun or moon, caused by the refraction of light through ice crystals in the atmosphere.

MOON: From the name of the earth's only natural satellite, which orbits the planet.

SHADOW: From the word for a dark image cast when an object moves in front of a light source (as in a lunar eclipse).

RORY: From the Gaelic name Ruaidri, meaning "great red king."

ROWAN: From the Irish Gaelic name Ruadhan, meaning "little redhead."
Alternate spellings: Roan, Rowen.

ROYAL: From the word for someone who is a king, a queen, or a member of their family.

RUMI: From Jalal ad-Din Muhammad Rumi, a thirteenth-century Persian poet.

RUNE: From the word for a symbol of mysterious or magical importance.

RYAN: From a Gaelic word meaning "king."

RYE: A nickname of Ryan (see above), it is also the name of a grain.

RYLAN: A variation of Ryan (see above).
Alternate spelling: Rylen.

Five Gender-Neutral Names Inspired by Grains

BARLEY: From the name of a cereal grass.

FARRO: From the name of a type of hulled wheat.

MAIZE: From the Spanish word for "corn."

MILLET: From the name of a group of small-seeded grasses.

TEFF: From the name of an ancient grain grown in Ethiopia and Eritrea.

Chapter Nineteen

Names That Begin with "S"

SAAR: From a Hebrew word meaning "tempest" or "storm."

SABBATH: From the name of a day of religious observance.

SACHA: A nickname of Alexandra (a Slavic name meaning "warrior's protector" and Alexandros (a Greek name meaning "protector of men").
Alternate spellings: Sascha, Sasha.

SAGE: From the name of a Mediterranean plant known for its silvery leaves and savory taste; the word sage can also mean "wise." Additionally, burning sage is a centuries-old tradition used to clear negative energies and bring in fresh energy.

SAILOR: From the word for someone who works on and/or knows his way around a boat.
Alternate spelling: Saylor.

SAKAE: From a Japanese name that, depending on the character used, means "prosperity" or "is brilliant."

SAKARI: There is debate over the origin of this name, which might come from the Sanskrit word *sarkara*, meaning "sugar," or from the Hebrew name Zcharya, meaning "the Lord recalled."

SALEM: An abbreviation of Jerusalem, this name comes from *salim* or *salīm*, the Arabic word for "safe," "secure," "perfect," or "complete."

SAM: Short for Samuel and Samantha, both of which come from the Hebrew name Shemuel, meaning "God heard."

SAMAR: From an Arabic expression meaning "night talk."

SAMI: From an Arabic word meaning "exalted." Also a nickname of Samuel and Samantha, both of which come from the Hebrew name Shemuel, meaning "God heard."
  Alternate spellings: Sammy, Samy.

SANG: From a Korean word meaning "enduring."

SANTANA: From a Spanish expression meaning "Saint Ana."

SAWYER: This English surname identifies a person who saws wood for a living.

SCIENCE: The word for the study of the physical and natural world.

SCOUT: The word for a soldier sent out ahead to gather information. Also the name of the astute young narrator in Harper Lee's *To Kill a Mockingbird.*

SEA: Another word for the ocean, the expanse of salt water that covers much of the earth's surface.

SEAN: From an Irish Gaelic name meaning "God's grace."
Alternate spelling: Shawn.

SELBY: An English surname that comes from the Old Norse words *selja*, meaning "willow," and *býr*, meaning "farm" or "settlement."

SENECA: One of five nations of the Native American Iroquois people who inhabited what is now upstate New York. Also the name of a Roman philosopher, Seneca the Younger.

Five Gender-Neutral Baby Names Inspired by Stars

ALTAIR: The name of this white dwarf star is derived from an Arabic phrase meaning "flying eagle."

PLEIADES: A star cluster that's part of the Taurus constellation.

POLARIS: Another name for the North Star.

SUHAYL: The Arabic name for Canopus, a white giant that is the second brightest star in the night sky.

VEGA: This bright blue white dwarf star is the fifth brightest in the night sky.

SENEGAL: From the name of a West African country.

SEQUOIA: From the Cherokee word *tsikwaya*, meaning "sparrow." Also the name of a tree, as well as a famous Native American leader.
Alternate spelling: Sequoyah.

SEREN: From a Welsh word meaning "star."

SETH: From a Hebrew word meaning "appointed."

SEVEN: Based on the word for the number, which has a long history of significance, from the seven days of the week to the seven wonders of the world.

SHAI: From an Aramaic word meaning "gift."
Related names: Shia, Shya.

SHALOM: From a Hebrew word meaning "peace."

SHANE: A variation of the Irish Gaelic name Sean, meaning "God's grace."
Alternate spelling: Shayne.

SHAW: From the Old English word *sceaga*, meaning "wood."

SHAY: From the Gaelic name Seaghdha, meaning "admirable."
Alternate spellings: Shea, Shaye.

SHELBY: From the Old Norse word *selja*, meaning "willow."

SHERIDAN: From the Irish Gaelic name Sirideain, meaning "seeker."

SHILOH: From a Hebrew expression meaning "his gift."

SHORE: From the word for the land along the edge of a body of water.

Five Gender-Neutral Celebrity Baby Names

BODHI: The name of the son of the actors Brian Austin Green and Megan Fox, as well as the singer Bobby Brown's daughter.

LINCOLN: The name of the daughter of the actors Kristen Bell and Dax Shepard.

MASON: The name of the actor Kelsey Grammer's daughter, as well as the reality star Kourtney Kardashian's son.

PHOENIX: The name of Spice Girl Melanie Brown's daughter and also of fitness guru Jillian Michaels's son.

WYATT: The name of the daughter of the actors Mila Kunis and Ashton Kutcher and also of the singer Sheryl Crow's son.

SHURA: A nickname of Alexandra (a Slavic name meaning "warrior's protector" and Alexandros (a Greek name meaning "protector of men").

SIDNEY: From the Old English phrase *sidan eg,* meaning "wide island" or "wide meadow."

SILVER: From the English word for the soft, luminous white metal used in jewelry and other decorative items.

SINCLAIR: From Saint-Clair, the name of a village in northern France.

SKY: From the word for the air above; also a nickname of Skyler (see below).
  Alternate spelling: Skye.

SKYLER: From the Dutch word *schuiler,* meaning "fugitive."
  Alternate spellings: Schuyler, Skylar.

SLATE: After the English word for the flat gray rock used in roofing, flooring, and the phrase "clean slate."

SLOAN: From an Irish surname derived from a word meaning "raider."
  Alternate spelling: Sloane.

SNOW: From the white, fluffy precipitation that falls in winter in parts of the world.

SOL: From the Spanish word for "sun."

SOLACE: From the word meaning comfort or consolation.

SOLARIS: From a Latin word meaning "of the sun."

SORREL: From a word meaning a bright chestnut color; also the name of an herb.
Alternate spelling: Sorrell.

SOUTH: From the word for a direction, the opposite of north on a compass.

SPARROW: From the name of a songbird that was a favorite of Aphrodite, the Greek goddess of love.

SPENCER: From an English word meaning "dispenser [of provisions]."
Alternate spelling: Spenser.

SPRUCE: From the name of an evergreen tree.

STARLING: From the name of the songbird with iridescent feathers.

STEEL: From the name of an incredibly strong metal alloy.
Alternate spelling: Steele.

STELLAR: From a word meaning "related to the stars" or "outstanding."

STERLING: From an Old English word meaning "little star." It is also the description of silver that is 92.5 percent pure.

STEVIE: A nickname of Steven, Stephanie, or Stevland that comes from the Greek name Stephanos, meaning "crown" or "garland." Famous Stevies include the singers Stevie Nicks and Stevie Wonder.
Alternate spelling: Stevey.

STORM: From the name of a weather event that usually brings a combination of rain, snow, thunder, lightning, and wind.

STORY: From the word for a tale or anecdote.

STRONG: From the word for being able to withstand extreme pressure or external forces.

SULLIVAN: From a Gaelic expression meaning "dark eyes."

SUNG: From a Korean word meaning "successor."

SUTTON: An English surname for people originally from the "south settlement."

SUZU: From a Japanese name that, depending on the character used, means "cool," "star," or "pearl."

SWEDEN: From the northern European country of the same name.

SWEENEY: A surname of Irish and Scottish origins.

Chapter Twenty

Names That Begin with "T"

TAHOE: The name of this Nevada lake comes from the Native American Washoe word *tahoe*, meaning "big water."

TAI: From a Vietnamese word meaning "talented."

TAIWO: From a Yoruba expression meaning "have the first taste of the world."

TAIYE: An alternate form of Taiwo (see above).

TAJ: From a Sanskrit word meaning "crown."

TAL: From a Hebrew word meaning "dew."

TAMAR: From an English expression meaning "wide river."

TAO: From a Vietnamese word meaning "apple." In Chinese, it means "way" or "route" and is the name of the underlying principle of the universe.

TARAN: From a Gaelic word meaning "thunder."
Alternate spellings: Taren, Taryn.

TATE: From the Old English name Tata, meaning "cheerful."

TATUM: From an Old English word meaning "Tata's homestead."

TAY: A nickname of Taylor, which comes from the Norman French word *taillier*, meaning "to cut."
Alternate spelling: Taye.

TAYLEN: A more modern name with no clear meaning, this sounds like a mash-up between Taylor and Dylan.
Alternate spellings: Talyn, Taylin.

TAYLOR: From the Norman French word *taillier*, meaning "to cut" (see above).

TEAGAN: A variation of Teague, which comes from a Gaelic expression meaning "wise poet."
Alternate spellings: Teagen, Tegan.

TEAL: From the word for a small freshwater species of duck and also a shade of light blue-green.

TEDDY: Traditionally a nickname of Theodora and Theodore, which come from Theodorus, a Greek name meaning "God's gift."

TEMPLE: From the word for a place of worship, probably a surname given to those working in or living near a temple.

TEMPO: From the word for the speed at which music is played.

TENNESSEE: From the name of the southern American state known for whiskey and bluegrass and country music.

TERRAN: From a word meaning "person of the earth" ("terra"). *Alternate spellings:* Terren, Terrin, Terin.

TEXAS: After the southern state that borders Mexico, its name is thought to come from the Caddo and Hasinais Native American word *tejas*, meaning "friends" or "allies."

Five Gender-Neutral Baby Names That Are Also US States

ARIZONA: From the southwestern state of the same name, home to Grand Canyon National Park.

DAKOTA: This name is connected with North and South Dakota and comes from the Native American tribe of the same name.

INDIANA: From the midwestern state of the same name. Made popular by the movie character Indiana Jones.

MONTANA: From a Latin expression meaning "mountain," this is also the name of a western US state.

NEVADA: From a Spanish word meaning "snowfall," this is also the name of a southwestern US state.

THAMES: After the river Thames in England, which is thought to come from the Sanskrit word *tamas*, meaning "dark," or perhaps from the Roman words *tam*, meaning "wide," and *isis*, meaning "water."

THANH: From a Vietnamese word meaning "brilliant consummation."

THEMBA: From a Xhosa word meaning "hope."

THEO: A nickname of the Greek name Theodorus, meaning "God's gift."

Five Gender-Neutral Names Inspired by Wanderlust

FINN: From Mark Twain's classic character Huckleberry Finn, who travels the Mississippi River on a raft.

JOURNEY: From the word for a trip—because it's all about the journey, right?

MARLOW: From the Old English phrase *mere lafe*, meaning "driftwood."

MEANDER: From the word for following a winding course, this name rhymes with the Greek Leander.

ROAM: From the word for traveling aimlessly, this name conjures up an adventurous spirit.

THISTLE: From the name of a weedy plant that has prickly leaves and purple flowers.

THUNDER: From the name of the loud noise that comes from the expansion of rapidly heated air in the sky, usually following a lightning flash.

TIERNAN: From the Irish Gaelic name Tighearnach, meaning "lord."

TIERNEY: A variation of Tiernan (see above).

TIMBER: Evoking the names Tim and Kimberly; also a nod to the wood made from trees for building.

TOBY: A nickname of Tobias, an English name based on the Hebrew name Tuvya, meaning "God is good."
Alternate spellings: Tobey, Tobie.

TONY: A nickname of the names Anthony and Antonia.
Alternate spellings: Toni, Tonie.

TRAVELER: From the word for one who travels.

TRISTAN: An Ancient Celtic name derived from the name Drostan and influenced by the French word *triste*, meaning "sad."
Alternate spellings: Tristen, Tristin, Tristyn, Trystan.

TRUE: From the word meaning "accurate" or "reflecting reality."

TRUST: From the word for believing in someone or something.

TULLY: From a Gaelic word meaning "quiet" or "peaceable."
Alternate spelling: Tulley.

TUPELO: A type of tree and honey, and also a city in Mississippi. The name comes from the Native American Creek word *topiló*, meaning "swamp tree."

TYLER: From an English word meaning "worker in roof tiles."
Alternate spellings: Tylar, Tyeler.

TYSON: From Tison, an Old French name meaning "high-spirited."

Chapter Twenty-One

Names That Begin with "U"

UMBER: A short form of Umberto and Umberta, which come from the ancient Germanic phrase *hun berht*, meaning "famous giant" or "famous warrior." It is also the name of a natural brown pigment.

UNE: From a West African Akposso word meaning "road."

Five Gender-Neutral Names Inspired by Crayon Colors

CERULEAN: A sky blue.

INDIGO: A dark-blue color, like the dye that comes from the indigo plant.

PERI: After periwinkle, a pale lavender-blue that gets its name from the periwinkle plant.

SILVER: A cool metallic, named for the precious metal that has long been used for currency, jewelry, and household goods.

TEAL: A shade of light blue-green, as well as the name of a small freshwater species of duck.

UPTON: From an English word meaning "upper settlement."

URBAN: From the Latin name Urbanus, meaning "city dweller."
Alternate spelling: Urbain.

URI: From a Hebrew word meaning "flame."

UTAH: After the western US state, notable for its desert landscape and Great Salt Lake.

Chapter Twenty-Two

Names That Begin with "V"

VAL: From the Latin name Valentinus, meaning "strong" or "healthy."

VALE: From a poetic name for a valley.

VALEN: A nickname of Valentine, from the Latin name Valentinus, meaning "strong" or "healthy."

VALO: From a Finnish word for "light."

VALOR: From the word for great courage.

VEGA: From the Arabic phrase *al nasr al waqi*, meaning "falling vulture"; in Spanish, a large valley or grassy plain.

VEGAS: A short form of Las Vegas, the Nevada gambling and entertaining mecca. In Spanish, the name of the city translates as "plains" or "meadows."

VERDI: From the surname of Italian opera composer Giuseppe Verdi. Also the first half of the word *verdigris*, which is the blue-green substance that can form on copper and other metals.

Five Gender-Neutral Names
Inspired by US Cities

BROOKLYN: From one of New York City's five boroughs (and arguably the hippest).

CAMDEN: From the historic harbor town in Maine.

DALLAS: From a northern Texas city made famous in the 1970s, '80s, and '90s by the nighttime soap opera of the same name.

ORLANDO: From the most magical place on Earth for Disney fans. This Florida vacation destination shares a name with a gender-bending book by Virginia Woolf and a movie of the same title.

SALEM: From Salem, Massachusetts. Beyond that, the name is an abbreviation for Jerusalem and comes from *salim* or *salim*, Arabic for "safe," "secure," "perfect," or "complete."

VERSE: From the word for writing that rhymes in a poem or song.

VESPER: From the word for a prayer or a reference to the "evening star," Venus.

VICTORY: From the word for triumph, success, or a win.

VRAI: From a French word that means either "elaborate" or "interesting" or "true" or "real," depending on where it is used in a sentence.

Chapter Twenty-Three

Names That Begin with "W"

WALKER: From the Old English word *wealcere*, meaning "cloth washer."

WALLACE: From the Old French word *waleis*, meaning "Welshman."
Alternate spelling: Wallis.

WESLEY: From an Old English expression meaning "western meadow."
Alternate spelling: Westley.

WEST: A direction and an English surname for families who lived west of an established settlement.

WHIT: A nickname of Whitney, which comes from the Old English word *hwit*, meaning "white."
Alternate spelling: Witt.

WILDE: From the Old English word *wilde*, meaning "untamed."
Alternate spelling: Wild.

WILDER: A variation on Wilde (see above).

WILEY: From an Old English expression meaning "crafty."

WIM: A Dutch nickname of William, from the ancient Germanic phrase *wil helm*, meaning "determined protector."
Alternate spellings: Whim, Whym.

WIN: Traditionally a nickname of Winston, from the Old English name Wynnstan, meaning "joyful stone"; also, the English word for success or triumph.

WINDSOR: From the Old English phrase *windels ora*, meaning "landing place with a winch."

WINTER: From the season that goes from the winter solstice (December 21) to the spring equinox (March 20) and features cold temperatures, snow, and ice in many regions.

WISDOM: From the word for knowledge and good judgment.

WOLF: From the German word for the wild animal.

WREN: From the name of a small brown songbird.

WYNNE: From the Old English name Wine, meaning "friend."
Alternate spelling: Wyn.

Chapter Twenty-Four

Names That Begin with "X"

XADRIAN: A modern riff on the name Adrian, from the Latin name Hadrianus, meaning "one from the city of Adria."

XAN: A very short form of Alexander or Alexandra, from the Greek name Alexandros, meaning "protector of men."

Five Gender-Neutral Names Inspired by Buddhism

BEAM: From a word meaning a sunbeam or ray of light.

BODHI: From a Sanskrit word meaning "enlightenment" or "awakening."

DAWA: From a word meaning "moon" or "Monday."

LOTUS: From the name of a flower that grows out of muddy water; it represents purity and spiritual awakening.

NIRVANA: From the name of the final goal of Buddhism, often synonymous with Heaven or an idyllic state.

XEN: An alternate spelling of Zen, a school of Buddhism that emphasizes meditation and intuition.

XUAN: An alternate form of Chun, which, depending on the tone and characters associated with this name, means "spring," "love," "life," "simple," "pure," or "honest."

Chapter Twenty-Five

Names That Begin with "Y"

YALE: From the Connecticut Ivy League University of the same name.

Five Gender-Neutral Baby Names Inspired by Video Games

JAYCE: From *League of Legends.* Traditionally a nickname of Jason, which comes from the Greek name Iason, meaning "healer."

HAINLEY: From *Mass Effect: Andromeda.* Possibly an alternate spelling of the German surname Heinle.

KAIDEN: From *Mass Effect 3.* Pronounce it like Kaden (from an Arabic word meaning "companion") or even like "shy den." (Kai is Hawaiian for "seawater," and in other parts of the world it comes from a Greek word meaning "Earth.")

RAIDEN: From *Mortal Kombat.* As with Kaiden, above, you could pronounce it like "rye-den" or "raid-en."

WYNNE: From *Dragon Age: Origins.* This name traces back to the Old English name Wine, meaning "friend."
   Alternate spelling: Wyn.

YARDLEY: An English surname that likely meant "of the yard."

YASIN: A name formed from the Arabic equivalents of the letters *y* and *s*, the first letters of the thirty-sixth chapter of the Quran, the primary sacred writing of Islam.

YOSHI: Depending on the Japanese character used, this name means "good luck," "righteous," "good," "virtuous," or "respectable." Gamers may know Yoshi as the dinosaur pal of Mario from *Super Mario World*.

YULE: From an Old English word meaning "Christmastime."

YURI: In Japanese, this name is represented by characters meaning "lily."

Chapter Twenty-Six

Names That Begin with
"Z"

ZAIRE: From the former name of the equatorial African country known as the Democratic Republic of the Congo.

ZAMI: From an Arabic name meaning "helper" or "supporter."

ZAN: From a Hebrew word meaning "nourished."

ZANE: Related to John, which comes from Yochanan, a Hebrew name meaning "God's grace."

ZEN: From a school of Buddhism that emphasizes meditation and intuition.

ZENITH: From the word meaning a point directly above a location, or the very top.

ZEPHYR: From the word meaning a soft, gentle breeze.

ZEREN: From *dzeren*, the Russian name for the Mongolian gazelle.

ZINC: From the name of the metal that is an essential nutrient for both plants and animals.

ZION: This name for the hill in Jerusalem where the city of King David was built has come to more generally represent the kingdom of Heaven.

ZURI: From a Kiswahili expression meaning "beautiful."

Five Gender-Neutral Baby Names Inspired by Former Geographical Names

CEYLON: What we know as Sri Lanka was called Ceylon (an English version of Ceilão, the name given to the country by the Portuguese).

EDO: Before it became Tokyo, the historic Japanese city was called Edo, which means "bay entrance" or "estuary."

SIAM: The former name of Thailand is thought to come from the Sanskrit word *śyāma*, meaning "dark."

VOLTA: Burkina Faso, in Africa, used to be known as Upper Volta.

ZANZIBAR: This African country merged with another and renamed itself Tanzania.

★ ★ ★ ★

Your Favorite Names

★ ★ ★ ★

Your Favorite Names

About the Author

Melanie Mannarino is a freelance writer and editor. She spent the bulk of her career editing digital and print content for national media brands including *Real Simple* and *Cosmopolitan*. She has held staff positions at *Shape*, *Redbook*, *Marie Claire*, and *Seventeen*, as well as at Weight Watchers International, where she served as director of content for the United States, and executive editor of *Weight Watchers Magazine*. Career highlights include judging *Iron Chef America: Battle Broccoli*, writing the dating advice book *The Boyfriend Clinic*, and skipping out on a brunch check with the actor David Duchovny.

Melanie is a longtime fan of gender-neutral names, having named her beloved childhood doll "Meat and Potatoes." She lives in New Jersey with her husband, son, and two cats, Tiger and Lola (both girls).